MEDITATION

SELF LOVE

MINDFULNESS

The Fundamental Guide to
Dealing with Anxiety, Developing
Emotional Intelligence, and
Listening to Your Inner Voice - A
Self Help Book For True Happiness
and Freedom

ASHLEY R. BROWN

ISBN - 9798365463912

TABLE OF CONTENTS

INTRODUCTION

Finding your way to emotional intelligence and lessening the burden of anxiety can feel like an insurmountable obstacle. Many people mistakenly believe that concepts like emotional IQ and even intuition are things that some people are born with and cannot be learned. They believe that the only people who are able to get in touch with their inner voice and make good use of their gut feelings are those who are blessed not to have emotional reactions to the hardships of life. However, the truth is that you can cultivate these skills with a lot of hard work through practices like meditation, self-love, and mindfulness.

Practices like meditation and mindfulness set the stage for you to tune into your emotions but that is not all they offer. It is a way to distance yourself from those emotions, even for just a few minutes during the practice and exercises that you will find within the pages of this book. Once you can gain some perspective and peace from the onslaught of emotional turbulence, you have a much better chance of recognizing the gut instinct that seems to come so naturally to some people. The truth is that intuition is there for everyone, but you may not be trained to tune into it in the right way. Once you learn how to identify the inner voice that has been there all along, you will discover more happiness and true freedom in your day-to-day life.

Even simple practices like self-love can help you cultivate this feeling of happiness and freedom. Expressing compassion for yourself is a core part of how you feel about yourself as a person and what you need to do next. Take a break from social media and the constant need to compare yourself to others, and start embracing your desire to be wholly yourself. The minute that you allow yourself to be who you truly are, you will discover that there is tangible freedom for you to be the person you want to become in the days and years ahead. It is an incredibly personal path to success in this area, but there is no doubt that anyone can master a sense of self-love.

If you have ever found yourself doubtful that happiness and freedom are your birthrights, then you may need to tune into some of the exercises found in this book. We will dive deeper into the science behind some of these concepts like meditation, self-love, and mindfulness, and we will show you just how to cultivate these practices in your daily life. Nothing takes more than a few minutes to implement, but it can have far-reaching effects on your mood, your professional life, and even your relationships with your friends, partners, and coworkers.

Decide where you want to start and get in touch with your thoughts and feelings in a way that promises not to let you get overwhelmed by the volume of thoughts or the intensity of your emotions. This is a great way to ease into the practices that can shape your future, help you to find clarity for your inner voice, and ultimately lead to true happiness. If this is something that appeals to you right here and now, then you need to learn some of these practices. Let's get started so that you can tap into the freedom and happiness that everyone deserves to experience in abundant life. You will be glad that you took the leap and started today when you experience those feelings in the days and weeks ahead.

CHAPTER ONE

MEDITATION FOR ANXIETY

If you suffer from near-constant anxiety, you are likely familiar with the little voice in the back of your mind that constantly chatters to you. In fact, you are likely so used to it that you cannot put it in its place and would not be sure what to do with it if you were able to silence it. It constantly tells you just what you should be doing now, what you should have done, and what should happen next. The good news is that this inner voice can actually be silenced through the power of the simple act of meditation.

Meditation involves being extremely mindful of the ideas that float through your mind at any given time. The object is not to issue judgment on the thoughts you have but rather to simply acknowledge them, file them away, and move on. When you hear the word meditation, you may think about sitting on a cushion in an Indian ashram, legs folded up beneath you while incense burns in the background. While this is certainly true of some styles of meditation, you can still access the same powerful benefits of a regular practice from the comfort of your own home, no matter where that might be.

All you have to do is find a quiet place where you can relax, a place where you will not be bombarded by external stimuli vying for your attention. Find a comfortable seat, whether that means on the floor or in your desk chair. The only requirements are that you sit in silence and are willing to go deep beneath the surface-level thoughts to a place of peace where you can start to experience true happiness and calm. The silence is key to unlocking the benefits of meditation for yourself. It is thought that the mind is actually silent at baseline, though it may feel far from it when you struggle with anxious thoughts. Meditation is all about tapping into this more natural state of mind and harnessing that power for good.

There are several different types of meditation that you might encounter to experience quiet in both mind and body. One is mindfulness meditation, which we will go into in more detail in chapter three. Other types include spiritual, mantra, focused, movement, and loving-kindness. You can even go through progressive relaxation to get back into your body and out of your mind, which we will discuss in greater detail in the exercises at the end of this chapter.

Spiritual meditation is great for those who want to tap into their concept of a higher power. Many people do this through contemplative prayer, depending on their religious beliefs. Some feel more connected spiritually by meditating in a place of worship instead of in their home, though both are valid options for this type of meditation. Try focusing on a spiritual text as a sort of mantra and see what wisdom presents itself to you while you focus on quieting the inner voice.

If spirituality is not the right fit for you, mantra meditation is similar but without the religious connotations. You can instead focus on a phrase or image that features your intention for the practice. Some people like to repeat their mantra out loud while meditating, and this is one of the exceptions to the general rule that you should be silent during meditation. The repetition of a mantra can make you feel more deeply in touch with your environment and serves to increase awareness. For those who want to try meditation but struggle with staying focused, a mantra is a great theme that you can continue to return to throughout the practice.

Focused meditation is another type that you may want to sample if you are new to a meditation practice. Much like mantra meditation, this form is intended to engage your senses in such a way that it absorbs your thoughts and allows you to relax, quieting the inner mind. In place of a mantra that you repeat over and over again to yourself, you can instead count beads (such as a rosary or mala beads), listen to relaxing sounds like nature sounds, count your breaths, or light a candle. When you find that your mind is shifting back to the place of anxiety and worry, all you have to do is bring your attention back to the object that you are focusing on for the session.

Movement meditation goes beyond the practice of yoga, though this is a valid way to tap into the body. As you may have already guessed, movement meditation is designed to marry the mind and body together, allowing you to find peace while working within the present moment. It can be as simple as taking a walk and experiencing the sensation in the balls of the feet, the heels, and the legs. You might tend to your garden and mindfully feel the dirt beneath your fingers and smell the plants that surround you. Of course, there are other methods that allow you to tap into both body and breath such as tai chi. Movement meditation is ideal for those who experience somatic symptoms related to anxiety and want to cultivate a greater awareness of how their body feels when it is at peace.

Loving-kindness meditation is designed to make you feel better not only about yourself but also about those who are around you. During this type of meditation, you will focus your thoughts on the people closest to you, your friends, and your family. You will focus on wishing them love and good things from the universe. As you move through the people close to you, you can start to expand your circle to those you may not know well and eventually to all living beings. You can even extend that same loving-kindness to yourself and minimize the stress you feel due to your anxiety. If you are tied up in worry, particularly about your relationships, this is a great way to minimize some of that internal chatter.

Last but not least, there is also progressive relaxation. This is a common favorite because it is so easy to do on your own at home, at your desk at work, or during a commercial break. You will start by tensing as many muscles in the body as you can. Start at the feet and progressively move upward toward the crown of the head. At every stage of the body, take a moment to consciously relax those muscles and allow them to sink deeper into the floor, couch, or bed. Stop at the ankles, the calves, the knees, and so on all the way up to the face. The face should be relaxed one part at a time, starting with the jaw and moving toward the tongue, eyes, forehead, and even the cheeks. Move as slowly as you wish depending on how much time you have for this type of meditation. A guided version of progressive relaxation is easy to find on the internet if you prefer to have someone walk you through this type of exercise.

The truth is that it does not really matter what type of meditation you engage in. They all have the same desired effect: silencing the mind and the internal noise that often accompanies anxiety. It is a mindful practice that enhances your sense of emotional well-being, but that is not all that meditation has to offer its practitioners. It also increases your emotional intelligence. This is the measure that professionals use to determine how effectively you can identify your own emotions and the feelings of others, and how well you can manage and balance those emotions in your day-to-day life. Higher emotional intelligence does not necessarily mean that you are too sensitive. Instead, it means that you can recognize and pinpoint your feelings in the fastest way possible so that you can begin to self-soothe.

Meditation has been proven through numerous studies to actually change the structure of the brain in tangible ways. While it can certainly make you feel more spiritual and even more connected to the people in your life, it also changes the way your brain interacts with itself by altering neural pathways. This practice can redefine your relationship to your own personal emotional self-control that prevents you from responding to a situation out of anxiety. The amygdala becomes weaker with meditation while the prefrontal cortex becomes much stronger. The weakened amygdala is thought to be responsible for fight or flight responses while the prefrontal cortex is the home of both logic and reason.

Another perk of regular meditation practice is that it strengthens your empathy for others, particularly if you are practicing loving-kindness meditations. Even if this is not your preferred style of meditation, it still helps your emotional intelligence by allowing you to better tap into your own emotions and more easily recognize those same emotions in others. You will have a much easier time relating to others and understanding their mindset because you will be extremely cognizant of your own. This can improve your ability to resolve conflict as well.

Overall, meditation helps you to develop a greater sense of self-awareness. Some people refer to this as their gut instinct or their intuition. You will be more attuned to what is going on around you and within you, allowing you to experience a greater sense of peace. Not to mention, you will not be as prone to act on impulse as the prefrontal cortex is strengthened and helps you to make those difficult decisions that come up over the course of the day.

EXERCISES FOR BEGINNERS

If you believe that regular meditation practice could be the right move for your anxiety and feelings of overwhelm, then it might be time to try some of these practices. For all of the below exercises, make sure that you are seated somewhere comfortable, relaxing, and mostly quiet. If you are not seated on the floor, try to keep your feet rooted into the floor so that you have some connection with the earth. From here, you can try some of these simple meditation exercises to quiet the mind, improve emotional intelligence, and more.

BREATHING EXERCISES

Many people love to focus on the breath during their meditation practice. This type of focused meditation is easy because it involves no extra items, requires very little brain power, and can have a very powerful effect on your mood and your body. At the end of this exercise, you will likely feel that you are far more relaxed. Consider doing each of these exercises ten times through, but you can do them for longer if you like them or if time allows.

4-7-8 Breathing

This is one of the most straightforward ways to begin your meditation practice. From your seated position, all you have to do is inhale through the nose for a slow count of four. Hold your breath while you count to seven at the same rate. Extend your exhale through the mouth for a count of eight. If this feels too challenging for you at first, you can count faster until you become more experienced with holding your breath for a count of seven. Just remember that consistency is key: count at the same pace for inhalation, holding, and exhalation.

Counting the Breaths

For this type of exercise, you can either aim to count your first ten breaths or set a timer for your meditation practice. A five- to a ten-minute session is perfect for beginners who just want to feel a little relief from their anxiety. Take deep breaths but make them as natural as you possibly can, breathing in through the nose and out through the mouth. On each inhale, count the number of breaths you have taken so far. Slowly release your exhale and count again on the next inhale. See how high you can get before you lose track of where you were.

BODY EXERCISES

If you are having a difficult time with the sensations in your body and are holding a lot of your anxiety in the muscles of the body, you might want to consider a body exercise. Progressive relaxation is one type of body exercise, but there are others that may be more appealing to you. This is a great practice to have when you are feeling overwhelmed or for winding down in bed at the end of a long day. It will help you to identify any areas of the body that are holding tension or storing your anxiety.

Body Scan

This is a great exercise to practice while lying down, either on the floor or in the comfort of your bed if you plan to drift off to sleep after you finish. Once you are comfortable, close your eyes and take a deep breath. You can start with a round of progressive relaxation or dive headfirst into your body scan. Starting at the soles of your feet and working your way inch by inch to the top of the head, notice the sensation in each body part. Are you experiencing tension, pain, or any type of discomfort?

As you progress up the body, take a deep breath at each point where you might be feeling something less than pleasant. Allow that part of the body to re-lax, release the tension, and try to soothe the aches of that part. If it is hard to let go of the tension in a particular part of the body, you can try to tense it for a few seconds and then let it go. Pay attention to each major muscle group all the way from the feet up to the face.

VISUALIZATION

Another key exercise that you can do as part of a regular meditation practice is visualization. Chances are that you have some experience with this in the form of daydreaming, but this is a more focused practice that can help you to eliminate anxiety. You can visualize anything you want that brings a smile to your face and relaxation to your body. If you happen to be worried about a major presentation at work, you can picture yourself acing it and earning the praise of your boss. If you happen to be worried about a situation with your spouse, picture how it would go if it went as smoothly as you want it to.

There is no limit to what you can imagine with this type of meditation.

Another way that you can approach visualization is by imagining a place that brings you complete peace. It does not necessarily have to be a real place or even a place that you have been before. Some people like to picture the beach, the mountains, or even just a peaceful meadow. The important thing is that you immerse yourself as fully into the visualization as you possibly can. Close your eyes and try to really experience what it is like to be in the area that you are visualizing. Experience what you would see, touch, taste, smell, and hear while you are there or while you are going through a specific situation.

While you are feeling the sensations that accompany your visualization, it is common for people to feel their anxiety start to pop into their minds from time to time. Take a breath and note the feeling or sensation that it brings with it. Acknowledge the thought, and then exhale as you release it and the hold that it may have over your mind and body.

If you have trouble with visualization, there is another way to approach it: guided imagery. These recordings or readings take you on a journey to a peaceful place. They walk you through the process of letting go of your worries and thoughts as you journey through this place. You can find them recorded on the internet, can record them yourself as you read a script, or simply read through them, pausing at times to soak in everything that the meditation is bringing to you.

THE SIMPLE WAY

Of course, meditating does not have to be some long and complicated process. It can be as simple as developing more awareness of your feelings and anxieties in a tangible way. Find a seated position that makes you feel comfortable so you do not focus on any pain or discomfort during the practice. Inhale slowly through your nose, and exhale slowly through your mouth. Keep in touch with the thoughts that cross your mind and then slowly let each one of them float out of your mind, as a cloud floats through the sky on a windy day.

You can do this practice for as long as you like or keep it short and sweet. Most beginners start with a five- or ten-minute session but more experienced practitioners may prefer to stick to longer time-frames up to a half-hour. As you become more ex-perienced, it will be easier to sit for longer and to notice your thoughts passing you by.

No matter what type of meditation you choose to practice, one thing is certain: you will realize that your anxiety will not have the same grip on you that it used to. You will be able to let things go more eas-ily and will find yourself tapping into this feeling of calm on a regular basis. If you want to increase your emotional intelligence, lower your anxiety, and min-imize somatic symptoms in the body, these exercises are certain to put you well on your way to learning more about how to better manage your experience of anxiety.

CHAPTER TWO

HOW TO INSTILL MORE SELF-LOVE

Most people know what it means to love another person: caring for them, supporting them, and giving them the undivided attention that they need. Unfortunately, many people stop with this type of unconditional love before applying it to the self. Self-love is just as important as loving the other people in your life, but the concept is just a little bit different. If you know that your relationship with yourself feels a little rocky at times, then here is what you need to know about the concept of self-love and how you can apply it to yourself.

Self-love means that you accept yourself just as you are – your strengths, your likes and dislikes, even your weaknesses. You should demonstrate the same level of respect for yourself that you would extend to a close friend or family member. All of your thoughts toward your inner self or outer self should be judgment-free and full of kindness. Remember that you are a human being who is bound to make mistakes from time to time, but you do not have to define yourself by those mistakes. You should be focused on growing as a person, whatever that may mean to you. Self-love goes beyond just your outer actions though. It also means that your thoughts and even your feelings are geared toward your own health and well-being.

The goal of self-love is to nurture a positive view of the self as often as possible. While you may still have your own frustrations and hang-ups that leave you feeling less than pleasant about yourself, you should find a deep current of love underneath those unwanted feelings. For example, you might be angry at how you responded to a certain situation, but you can still feel love for yourself in the midst of those uncomfortable feelings. This is very similar to how many people love their spouse or their close friends. Disagreements are bound to happen, but the way they feel about that person beneath the surface is unaffected by the situation at hand.

Try to think of loving yourself the same as you would another person. Once you know how to love and empathize with another person, you will have a much greater understanding of how to love yourself. It can be as simple as motivating yourself with positive thoughts, extending forgiveness for mistakes, and meeting your own needs. Think about all of the ways that you love the people in your life and then experiment to see what it would feel like to extend those same courtesies to yourself. You can be assertive to get your needs met, release the anger that might be simmering beneath the surface, and follow up on your goals. Self-love is all about helping you to live your very best life and increasing your happiness.

How does the act of self-love increase your overall happiness? It is actually quite simple once you realize that the concepts found here are not all that revolutionary. Because self-love is designed to promote your own wellbeing, just as you would that of a friend or family member, you can prioritize your needs and desires. By pursuing those things that make you feel most fulfilled, you will experience more happiness in your day-to-day life.

First, self-love enables you to live your life according to your values. If you prioritize your family as one of your core values, then you will spend more time with them. By putting things in their proper place, you will have a great understanding of how to give yourself what you need in order to live out those values. When you find yourself snapping at your family or getting involved in more and more arguments, it might be time to press pause and do something that nourishes you. Be sure to survey your current life and find areas where you may not be living up to those values that you hold dear. It might be time to implement a little more self-love so that you can better live according to the values that mean the most to you.

Second, self-love also has an intrinsic effect on your overall confidence. Once you tap into the things that mean the most to you and prioritize your desires, you are bound to feel a surge in how confident you feel. As you practice self-love over the long haul, you will start to trust your instincts more and more. Insecurity is pushed to the side, you are gentler with yourself, and you will learn to fully embrace who you are and whom you were created to be. As you increasingly grow more confident, the natural effect is that you will be happier with your daily life. Showing a little bit of compassion toward yourself can go a really long way toward building confidence.

Another way that self-love can promote happiness is through resilience. The truth is that no matter how much self-love you practice, there will be hard times ahead. It is simply a natural part of life that is unavoidable for anyone and everyone. Challenges will arise and you will have to rise up to meet them.

The good news is that if you have been practicing self-love for a while, then you have a leg up on what those challenges will bring into your life. You are used to playing up your strengths, issuing compassion toward yourself, and embracing opportunities for growth. Instead of being beaten down by hard times, you will see them as great opportunities to practice living according to your values whether that means prioritizing yourself, setting boundaries, or something else entirely. It boosts your overall level of resilience. The amount of self-love you have for yourself can often be used to predict how well you will bounce back from hardships.

The good news is that practicing self-love doesn't have to be a complicated endeavor. There are a few simple actions you can take to boost your happiness in this capacity. Remember that self-love starts with you, so you will need to put time and effort into adopting some of these practices that can make you feel more secure, confident, and resilient over time. Here are a few ways that you can start to implement self-love quickly – though we must warn you, it may not come naturally or easily to you at first. Your ability to fully participate in these actions will grow over time.

Most people are familiar with the phrase that comparison is the thief of joy. We naturally want to give into competition with those closest to us. Who has the nicest car? The nicest house? The best education or a well-paying job? We often hold ourselves up to the people closest to us as a standard for how we are doing in our own lives. Unfortunately, this type of direct comparison can leave you feeling worse about yourself because there will always be someone who has something better than you do, whether that means a job or a tangible belonging. Instead of trying to keep up with Joneses, try to focus on your own path to success without comparison to anyone else.

Another way to implement self-love is to have compassion for yourself. You know that you are bound to make mistakes from time to time, but how do you respond when that happens? This is one of the ultimate tests of self-love. Instead of berating yourself for those mistakes, it is time to give up the harsh self-talk. Give yourself some grace when something does not go according to plan. Embrace the mistakes that you make and try to find opportunities for growth through them. This helps you to keep your vision on the future instead of being blinded by your past and the mistakes that you made before.

Self-love also means that you need to set some boundaries with people in your life. You should have clear lines drawn about who can call you in the middle of the night, whom you will allow to hear your deepest secrets, and who might need to be placed at a greater distance. Not everyone you meet is worthy of being placed in your inner circle. Think about who has earned the right to be considered one of your closest friends and impose stricter boundaries for people who drain you of your energy. Those people in your life that you consider to be toxic to your mental health should be given the boot from your life, regardless of how difficult this may be for you. Having self-love means that you are catering to your own needs and do not have time and space to cater to the feelings of people who are not worthy of your time.

Along the same lines, self-love means that you are putting yourself first. Too many times, we get caught up in the drama that other people bring into our lives and we neglect ourselves. It is time to put this habit firmly in the past. While it is okay to think of others and not to become completely selfish, remember that you need to recharge and decompress if you want to function at your absolute best. Without this time for yourself – whatever that might look like for you – you are putting yourself at risk of burnout. Self-love encourages you to put yourself first so that you can prioritize your mental wellbeing. Find hobbies and activities that refresh you and spend more time engaged with them so that you can care for others the way you desperately desire to.

As you spend more time recharging yourself, it is important to note that you can feel whatever feelings come to the surface. Part of embracing yourself and experiencing self-love is that you will be able to feel as much as possible, whether that is good or bad. You will find that you can press into those feelings and how they will help you to understand yourself, even if they feel uncomfortable in the moment. Even positive emotions have something to teach you: what you enjoy, what you need more of in your life, and a better understanding of who you are as a person. You do not have to define yourself by your feelings, but you should feel free to feel as much of them as you possibly can.

HOW TO PRACTICE SELF-LOVE

While the ideas above are great in theory, you might be wondering how you can start to practice self-love right away. Fortunately, there are tons of ways that you can start to take better care of yourself. They do not have to take much time or energy, and they can restore and refresh your spirit. Ultimately, these five simple acts of self-love can help you to feel more at peace and in touch with who you are.

1. *Implement a Ritual You Love*

It is easy to get swept up in the hustle and bustle presented to us by the media day after day. You are constantly scanning the news channels, are absorbed by your favorite television shows, and are stuck in the endless scrolling of social media pages. Take a half hour and unplug from all of it. Some people may take this time to meditate, as we covered in the previous chapter. This is a great use of your time, but you can also create a different type of ritual that you love. Give yourself a massage, take a long bubble bath, or read a chapter from your favorite book. Find what nourishes you and engage in it for even a brief period.

2. Treat Your Body Well

A big part of self-love is accepting yourself exactly as you are. You should accept your body in all of its glory and flaws. This is not to say that you cannot strive to do better with your health, but it does mean that you should appreciate your body for all that it offers to you here and now. It gets you from point A to B. It is the reason you are able to work, play, laugh, and love. There are plenty of reasons to love your body, even if it does not look the way you want it to right now. All of this is to say that an act of self-love is to treat your body well.

Feed it foods that give you energy and allow you to grow. Exercise to give yourself a boost and a rush of endorphins, even if that just means going on a walk through your neighborhood. Make a list of all the things you do like about your body and pin it somewhere you can see it and refer back to it when those thoughts of comparison threaten to rob you of your peace and joy.

3. Take a Social Media Break

We already mentioned that comparison is going to rob you of your joy in the present moment. That might mean that you need to take a hard pass on visiting places that promote this type of comparison among your friends and family. In other words, social media platforms should be limited if you find yourself engaged in this type of comparison. Take a break for a few days or a couple of weeks to see if it makes a difference in how you feel about yourself. If you find that you feel much better after an extended absence, consider what it would look like to put a permanent ban on social media or strictly limit the amount of time you spend scrolling on your phone.

4. Find a Happy Place

Where do you feel absolutely at peace and ready for anything that might come your way? For some people, they feel happiest when they are at the seashore with their toes in the sand. Others might prefer a mountain hike, strolling through a museum, or having a picnic in a beautiful meadow. No matter what matters most to you, find a place that makes you happy and allows you to enjoy yourself. While you are here, take the time to relish the moment. This is a great time to meditate if you can by closing your eyes and absorbing the feeling of the sun on your skin, a favorite food on your tongue, and the smell of nature all around you. You can even do a moving meditation as you focus on the feeling of walking from one place to another, steadying your breath while you do so.

5. Boost Your Self-Esteem

Self-love does not always mean that you will have the highest self-esteem, but the two concepts are often closely related. If you are feeling a little down on yourself, do something that you know you are good at and something that you thoroughly enjoy. Whether that means baking a cake, painting a picture of a sunset, or going for a long run, you should do something that will boost your self-esteem. As you feel better about yourself, it will be that much easier to practice some of these other self-love habits that can make you feel more peaceful and happier in the moment.

CHAPTER THREE
MINDFULNESS FOR BEGINNERS

While meditation can help you to get in touch with your inner voice and intuition, mindfulness offers another powerful way to reconnect with yourself and your surroundings. The actual concept of mindfulness is not all that hard to understand. It is simply the act of being present in the moment, focused on what you are doing, feeling, and experiencing at that time. Meditation can help you to sink into your body to experience this phenomenon of mindfulness, but there are other ways to notice how you feel as well. The definition of mindfulness is quite simple, but the practice of it can be extraordinarily difficult for some people.

When you practice mindfulness, it is common for your thoughts to stray to whatever may be on your mind at that moment. This is an important part of the process, but you must learn the proper ways to deal with those thoughts. It should be enough at this moment to acknowledge them and then to let them pass by you. There is no need to react to them, respond to them, or act on them in any way. Noticing them is the only important part of the process here and now. Does this sound a little bit familiar? That is likely because meditation encourages mindfulness, so you are already starting to practice some of these excellent habits.

Much like meditation, there are several different types of mindfulness practices that you can engage in. Some people like to practice mindfulness much like meditation by either sitting in a comfortable position with the eyes closed or through movement such as going on a walk, practicing yoga, or taking a jog. Of course, you can also insert mindfulness into your day-to-day life. Being absorbed by the taste of your food, enjoying the brilliant colors of a sunset, or painting a picture can all be great ways to infuse more mindfulness into your routine. It takes just a few minutes to bring awareness into the present moment, and nobody has to be any wiser that you are doing it. It is something that you do just for yourself, but the benefits of mindfulness are quite far-reaching.

The first and most prominent feature of someone who practices mindfulness is that they tend to have lower stress levels. By being present in the moment and surrendering to their thoughts and feelings, they are able to get a clearer idea of what is going on in their life. This can give quick clarity on what you should do next, particularly if you have some major decisions to make. When done regularly, a mindfulness practice can clue you into your inner voice and make it more likely that you will recognize your opinions, thoughts, and the path you should take moving forward.

As a related side effect of mindfulness, you also tend to get better performances. It is true that you might know what to do next, but you will also have increased clarity on how to go about that next thing. In other words, you will gain insight into what path to take because you will have some emotional separation from the situation at hand. Even if the situation is not loaded with emotional reverberations, you can still gain some clearer insight into exactly what needs to occur next which can boost your overall performance. It might even help you to stick with a challenging situation longer than you would otherwise think possible because you can separate the emotions that you feel from your actions.

However, the largest benefit of mindfulness is that it enhances emotional intelligence. This makes it more likely that your relationships will flourish and thrive, transforming you into an excellent friend, coworker, or partner. It makes you more empathetic because you will have your finger on the pulse of your own feelings. As you come to understand yourself more and more while you practice mindfulness, it will be easier to apply the insights that you gain to others. This gives you a deeper understanding of their inner workings by tuning into their body language, tone of voice, and even their facial expressions. You will be surprised at just how quickly you become more adept at reading the room, strengthening your relationship with everyone you come in contact with.

Along the same vein, you will also have an easier time managing difficult conversations. It is a fact of life that you will eventually encounter conflict whether at home or in a professional setting. When these situations arose in the past, you might have felt overwhelmingly frustrated, angry, or upset. This is frequently because you are so absorbed in your own reaction to the talk that you cannot think beyond it to see what could be gained from the information shared. Instead of getting stuck in the spiral of doom that often encounters these hard talks, you can notice the emotions you experience and let them go. It strengthens the prefrontal cortex in the brain, the area that is known for rationalizing and making logical decisions. You will be more likely to relate to the person you are talking to, less likely to respond from an emotional perspective, and will ultimately find that these talks are not as challenging as they have once been.

Part of this solution to difficult conversations is that you will have increased compassion for the people around you. It starts internally though. Mindfulness permits you to observe your emotions and then let them go. You can have compassion for yourself for what you feel, and this begins to extend to other people as well. You can more easily lend a supportive hand to the people you work with, to your spouse, and even to your children. Because you have more empathy for the people around you, you are also likely to want to help them through the things that seem to be troubling them. This leads your compassion muscle to stretch and grow. In turn, this deepens your relationships one at a time as they learn that they can depend on you to help instead of turning it into a conversation about your own emotional needs.

As we have already touched on, mindfulness makes it easier for you to tune into your inner voice. Sometimes, you might hear this referred to as your intuition or your gut instinct. This is because you are creating a bit more space in your mind and in your body for your deeper sense of knowing to shine through. Your emotions and even your physical feelings are key indicators of what your internal voice is trying to share with you. Notice what you feel and then see what your body and mind want you to do with that information. It might be as simple as taking thirty seconds to respond to a request, taking an hour to intuit what your next career move should be, or taking a weekend just to enjoy some space.

We will dive deeper into how to identify and listen to your inner voice in the next chapter, but for now, we will talk about making space for that voice to come to the forefront. First, you need to give it the space to come forward. You cannot simply keep trudging along with the daily grind and expect your intuition to beat you over the head. It needs quiet and peace to give you the clearest insight that it can give about what you should do next or how you should respond. Sometimes, you may not have five, ten, or even fifteen minutes to tune into your body. In this case, take a deep breath and pause just for a few seconds to see if you can tap into what you want or need to do at a deeper level.

Do not allow the mind to take over and rationalize what you should do next. The mind can trick you into doing something that may not be in your best interest, based solely on the emotions that you are feeling at the moment. While those emotions are always valid and should play a role in your decision-making process, you do not want to give them too much weight. If you do, you may find that you are less than thrilled about what you agreed to do as a result of your emotional reaction. Do not make long-term decisions based on short-term feelings.

The good news is that your inner voice or intuition likely has a few common ways of getting in touch with you. It is a little different for everyone, but you may come to recognize a still, small voice in the back of your head. Others might recognize a feeling in their gut or a greater sense of peace in their heart. For some people, intuition does come from a flash of emotion, but it is important to distinguish whether this will be a lasting feeling or whether it is fleeting. If you are unsure whether the feeling is bound to last as long as you need it to, then you may want to reconsider whether it is a good idea to make a decision at this moment. You can always excuse yourself to go to the restroom or to take a brief walk outside to clear your mind and search for inner knowing.

MINDFULNESS EXERCISES

If all of the benefits that you could reap from mindfulness are appealing to you, then you might be wondering just how you can start out with this practice. Much like meditation, it might take you a few tries to really tap into the space that allows you to be fully present. Start with shorter sessions and do not place too many expectations and rules upon yourself. Do your best to take note of your feelings and allow them to pass you by as you continue to focus on what you need to do in the present.

Mindful Eating

One of the best exercises to get you into your body and to start fostering a sense of mindfulness is to enjoy sensual pleasures as fully as you can. Eating is one of life's greatest joys so you may want to start with enjoying a delicious meal. Set aside a time where you can eat by yourself and savor every mouthful. Identify the tastes and seasonings of your food, notice the texture between your teeth, and make note of how the food feels against your tongue. No matter what you are in the middle of eating, you can note how it makes you feel.

If consuming a whole meal this way feels too overwhelming or you do not have enough time to eat a full meal, then try this trick instead. You can take a nugget of chocolate candy (a square from a chocolate bar, a Hershey's Kiss, or a fun-size candy bar). Place it on your tongue and then close your eyes. Note the way the candy tastes both initially and as the food begins to melt. Keep your attention on the taste and texture of the food until it eventually melts. This should take just a few minutes, so it is a much easier entry point for someone who is just sampling what mindfulness can do for them.

Falling Leaves

Are you struggling because you have so many thoughts and you just need to let them go so that you can think clearly about your next right thing? Mindfulness is much like meditation, but here is another exercise that you can try to eliminate some of these harsh thoughts. Find a comfortable seat, whether that means in your office chair or on the floor. You can even lay down if that makes you feel more comfortable. This is a great exercise to do as you are falling asleep at night so that you can have peaceful dreams.

Do your best to clear your mind at first. Then, allow your thoughts to drift back into your consciousness one at a time. Picture assigning that thought to a leaf on a large oak tree that is sitting right beside you. As you think about that thought, imagine that the leaf it is assigned to will drop slowly from the branches of the tree. The leaf will come closer and closer to the ground. When it lands, it is time to let go of that thought and reach for another. Continue doing this until you are able to sit quietly and your thoughts no longer pound at the door of your mind.

Another related exercise would be to assign your thoughts to rocks or sticks that are floating in a river. The rocks or sticks will float down the river with the current until they are out of sight – and out of mind. You can get creative with what and how you choose to acknowledge the thoughts that have been plaguing you. After a few minutes of any iteration of this exercise, you should be able to focus wholly on the present moment and allow your intuition to speak to you.

Take a Walk

Another great way to tune into what your body wants to share with you is to go for a walk. It would be ideal if you could walk outside, but pacing aimlessly around your house will work just as well for these purposes. If it is safe where you are, consider taking off your shoes while you walk so that you can feel more in tune with the sensations of your body. However, wearing shoes will not ruin your experience of this moving mindfulness practice so do not worry if it is not an option for you right now.

Start by taking one slow step. Exaggerate each movement so that you can feel each movement more fully. Focus on the way your weight shifts as you take a step, the way it feels on the ball of the foot, and how weight transfers from the heel to the ball of the foot. How do your arms move as you take each step? Can you feel the muscles on your legs contracting as you take one step after another? The goal is to be as much in your body as you can possibly be.

You should be so focused on how your body feels while moving that you find it hard to focus on your thoughts. If you do find that you have plenty of thoughts, try to let go of them with each new slow step forward. Take a brief moment to acknowledge them, feel the emotions that come with them, and then take a step as you encourage them to move away from the forefront of your mind.

Keep in mind that walking is not the only way you can tap into the body's mindfulness practice. You can do this with just about any physical activity. Try planting a few flowers in your garden, noting how the dirt feels underneath your fingernails. Go for a run and let each footstep pounding against the pavement represent another thought drifting from your mind until the only thing you can focus on is the breath. Cook a meal and enjoy the physical sensations of tasting while you cook, the heat coming from the stovetop, and the feeling of twirling around as you add ingredient after ingredient. Get creative and see how you can drop into the body and enjoy those sensations.

5-4-3-2-1

This is an exercise that therapists often give their patients when they are coping with anxiety and even panic attacks. However, it can be a useful skill for anyone who wants to gain mastery over their emotions and wants to be more fully present in the moment. This is a simple exercise that you can do with your eyes open. No one will even be wise to the fact that you are practicing your mindfulness when you are doing the 5-4-3-2-1 exercise. It grounds you right where you are and forces you out of your emotions, even for just a brief moment.

Start by naming five items you can see from where you are right now. If you happen to be in a very vibrant area, you can name more things until your mind starts to quiet down. The goal here is to name at least five and they can be anything: a desk, a lamp, a television, or even a cup of pens. The goal is to be observant of your surroundings, not to force you to come up with a creative response to the prompt.

From here, you will name four things you can touch. Feel the fabric of your shirt, the sturdiness of your chair beneath you, the solid floor under your feet, and the breeze drifting in through the open window. Pick up a pen and feel its weight in your hand. If you are at a loss for things that you can feel or touch, it could be as simple as noting how heavy or light your body feels at this precise moment.

Note three things you can hear, two things you can smell, and one thing you can taste. If you do not have anything in the vicinity that you can taste, think about what you might have recently had to eat or chew on. Maybe you can taste the aftertaste of your lunch because it had some strong onions. Perhaps you had a cup of strong black coffee and you can still imagine the taste that it left in your mouth. If you have to, get creative on some of these exercises.

Keep in mind that you can repeat this process as many times as you want to until you feel more present at this moment. It can be particularly helpful to try to find new answers to each of the prompts if you do this exercise two or three times in a row. By the time your mind tallies up all of the inputs you are asking it to go through, you will be at peace and will more readily be able to find access to that inner voice.

CHAPTER FOUR

GETTING IN TOUCH WITH YOUR INNER VOICE

A major part of recognizing what will make you happy long-term involves knowing yourself at a deep, almost cellular level. Everyone has an inner voice that tells them what they want, what they should pursue, and what they should leave behind. The problem is that many people do not know how to identify this voice, sometimes referred to as their subconscious. Distinguishing the characteristics of your inner voice is key if you want to know what would truly make you happy and grant you freedom from the stressors of your daily life as much as possible. You must learn how to recognize this voice, differentiate it from your intuition, and practice honing it if you want to achieve success in this area.

It all starts with establishing a regular practice of being able to listen to your inner voice. If you never spend any time trying to tap into this valuable aspect of your inner life, then you will never be able to experience the sensation of hearing what your body and mind really want from life. At the beginning of learning to distinguish this voice, you may need to spend lots of quiet time alone so that you can focus on what your mind, body, and spirit are trying to tell you. The best way to do that is through meditation or mindfulness practices that enable you to be more present and give you the space needed to focus on what you want or what you need to do next to achieve a state of happiness and freedom.

Fortunately, it does not have to require hours of solid concentration time to achieve a state where you can finally hear that inner voice. A few minutes here and there can add up and make distinguishing your subconscious clearer. As you gain more practice with your meditation or mindfulness practice, you may be able to spend less and less time in these states and still tap into your inner voice. It is a practice that you can bring with you anywhere you go. Just close your eyes, take a deep breath, and sink beneath the surface of your conscious mind to hear what you need to do next in any given situation. You will be able to hear the inner voice when you are taking a walk, washing the dog, or even while you are showering. It becomes a practice for you to listen to what your body is trying to tell you.

Another way that you can help define what you need to know or do next is by listening to your body. Do a quick body scan to see what you are feeling right now. Are you holding tension in the shoulders that might signal stress? Maybe you have a pounding tension headache from the onslaught of emotions that you are feeling. You could be overly exhausted from a trying day at work, have a stuffy nose, or even be dealing with issues related to your digestion. All of these feelings can clue you into what your body needs at this moment. Physical cues can be powerful means of showing you what to do next because emotions often present themselves somatically.

On the other hand, it is equally important to tap into your emotions. Be conscious of what you feel and whether it is aiding you at the moment or holding you back. Every emotion that you feel is a cue to take action. If you feel happiness (and we will talk more about this in the next chapter), it is a sign to keep on the path that you are already on. If you feel discontent, sad, angry, or disappointed, you might need to make some major changes and shake things up. Your intuition is heavily influenced by your emotions because they are vying for your attention.

One important thing to note about listening to your emotions is that you should not pass judgment on what you feel. It is easy to layer secondary emotions over your primary feelings when you start to feel shame or guilt for feeling a certain way. For example, you may feel angry at your spouse because they are not doing their fair share of the chores around the house. You do not want to be angry about it, so you feel shame for standing up for yourself with them. Anger is your primary emotion, and it is the one you should listen to you if you want to dive deep into your inner voice. Shame should be released and get no more of your attention.

When it comes to determining your inner voice, it gets easier with practice. Intuition often follows a similar pattern once you get used to hearing it. You might feel it deep in the gut as a sense that you should or should not do something. Other people experience an intense sensation of calm wash over their minds. There are no right or wrong ways to experience your inner voice, but knowing how it interacts with you is essential to recognize it more and more often in your life. It is the same as getting to know a new friend. You must invest time in getting to know your inner voice, studying how it speaks to you, and knowing the types of things that it shares with you.

Remember that it can be tempting to allow your conscious thoughts to overrule the sound of your inner voice. Oftentimes, we hear our inner voice but ignore it in favor of doing what we deem to be the logical thing. Our minds may not account for every aspect of a certain decision, and they may not take our feelings into consideration. Your inner voice is there for you at any and every turn, giving you the answers that matter most to you here and now. When you feel that prick of intuition, let it speak to you and ignore the reasoning of your mind that can lead you to feel conflicted and confused.

Of course, it is important to note the difference between intuition and your inner voice so that you have a better understanding of your experience with each one. While they are very similar concepts and we use them interchangeably here, you may notice a slight difference in how they manifest in your life. Knowing how both of them interact with and influence you can help you determine which one to follow when both are vying for your attention. The major difference between inner voice and intuition is simple: inner voice comes from conscious thought while intuition is more of a gut feeling based on emotion. But what does this look like in real life?

In real life, your inner voice is a thought that comes through the chaos of your mind and prompts you to do something. It could be a thought that you need to do something, a reminder of something similar, or even a thought that you would like to explore further at a later time. On the other hand, your intuition is more closely related to your feelings. This is the feeling that you experience deep in the stomach or the sense of peace that washes over you when you think about making the right decision. These messages tend to be shorter than those offered by the inner voice and they are a bit more to the point. Intuition tells you exactly what to do and when to do it while your inner voice sometimes meanders around the point. The inner voice may ask more questions while intuition offers a decisive answer.

While there are some slight differences between inner voice and intuition, they often have the same effect on you. When you are considering making a bold decision or even a more mundane one, they fill you with a sense of peace for the decision that lies ahead. Instead of the normal chaos of the mind while it weighs each and every option, inner voice and intuition allow you to feel calmer. It is a quiet type of energy that often fills people with a sense of calm, making it easier to do the next right thing.

If you are unsure whether you are hearing from your conscious mind or listening to your inner voice, evaluate the feeling that you get. Feelings of chaos or being pulled in multiple directions are probably your conscious mind at work. Feelings of peace that are centered in the heart or the gut are more likely to be the result of your inner voice or intuition. With some practice, you will easily be able to define where you feel each one and the sensation that goes along with it. To that end, we have a few exercises that you can practice to get better at learning to distinguish what your inner voice sounds like.

PRACTICES FOR HONING YOUR INNER VOICE

There are tons of ways that you can learn to tap into your inner voice and intuition, but you have to know where to start. You can get a leg up on intuition and inner voice by following some of these simple exercises. Try to practice them daily if you can, as this will strengthen the muscle and make it easier to tap into this resource when you really need it.

Daily Body Scans

With a meditation or mindfulness practice, you may have started with progressive relaxation where you go through each part of the body, one at a time. While the goal in these practices is to relax each body part until you reach a point of total bliss, a daily body scan is a bit different. In this exercise, you still want to call attention to every part of the body starting with the feet and working toward the crown of the head. However, your goal is not to relax the body but simply to note what you are feeling at each point.

When you start to feel tension, evaluate it and see if you can figure out where it is coming from. Holding any type of sensation or tension in the body is your intuition's way of sending you a message. If you are in the habit of performing these body scans daily, then you will recognize these messages much faster and may be able to resolve them sooner. This is a practice that is great right as you are getting ready to fall asleep, but doing it at several points throughout the day might be even more helpful. Try doing it more regularly if you have a major decision to make or are feeling lots of tension in the body that you think may be trying to tell you something.

Unplug for a While

In the modern age, you have messages coming at you from almost every angle. Between incessant work emails, the doom scrolls through social media, and the constantly-pinging texts from friends and family, you are bound to feel caught up in the moment all the time. With so many things fighting for your attention, it can be difficult to get quiet enough to hear from that small voice inside of you or the feeling in your gut. The best thing you can do, even for a short time, is to unplug from all of those messages.

When you have a major decision to make, consider doing a technology fast. Let friends and family know that you will be turning off your phone and surrendering your computer or tablet for a little while so that you can focus on what you need to do next in your life. While it would be great to do this for an extended time like a few days or a week, it might be more realistic to try introducing technology breaks for shorter stints at first. Try an hour, then two hours, and maybe even an entire day. The extra space and quiet that you will experience from being unplugged will allow you to focus on what you truly want and what will make you happiest.

Keep a Journal

Many people kept diaries as children but grew out of the habit as adults. Keeping a journal for the purposes of identifying your inner voice and intuition is a little different than simply recounting the events of your day. Instead of giving a surface-level overview, try to focus more on how your day made you feel and the things that are on your mind. You might want to start off by asking yourself a question that you have been grappling with in real life time and again. This gives you an opportunity to explore all sides of the issue and allows your intuition to come forth.

If writing is not the medium for you, fear not. There are plenty of other ways you can tap into the benefits of journaling without having to write page after page. Instead, you can also draw or make collages. Draw what you think the perfect outcome would look like, make an abstract drawing that represents your emotions, or anything else that comes to mind. Journaling can take whatever form you want it to take, so get creative with how you feel most in touch with your emotions.

Vision Boards

While this is one of the keys to manifestation, a vision board can also help you identify areas of improvement in your current life circumstances. Allow your inner voice to direct your thoughts and show you what the future could hold if you make that major decision that you have been putting off. Cut out pictures from magazines, scroll through Pinterest for the perfect images, or simply draw what you see when you think of your future. If an image floods you with a sense of peace for the decision that you are considering, it might be a flash of intuition and should make it onto your vision board.

Once your vision board is complete, it is easy to take a step back and admire what you imagine your future will look like. Then, close your eyes and sink deep into your body. What do you need to do right now to get to where you want to be? Allow your intuition to tell you the next decision that you need to take if you want to achieve that goal. Keep your vision board in a prominent place where you can see it and be reminded of what your inner voice is guiding you to do next.

Meditate

This book would be remiss if it did not point out one of the easiest and most obvious ways to tap into that inner voice or intuition: meditation. It allows your mind and body to get quiet and gives you the space to explore the emotions and decisions that come up for you. See chapter one for some specific exercises on how you can work meditation into your busy life.

Take Note of Dreams

Oftentimes, your subconscious reveals itself to you through dreams. Your mind is so hard at work trying to keep you afloat during the day that you are easily able to tune out your intuition. When you go to bed at night, your mind relaxes and your subconscious is able to come forward. This is a rich time for you to discover what may come next and how you feel about the decisions that you are presented with. If you really want to dig deep into what your dreams can offer you, try writing them down as soon as you wake up in the morning. This is the best way for you to reflect on what your subconscious mind has been trying to tell you all night long.

CHAPTER FIVE

FINDING HAPPINESS

C hances are that if you picked up this book, it is because you wanted to find freedom from your anxiety and uncover more happiness in your daily life. The good news is that happiness no longer has to be a fleeting emotion that you only feel from time to time. It can be a major component of your life instead. One of the easiest ways to cultivate that sense of happiness is through the regular practice of both mindfulness and meditation. How do these practices open your mind, heart, and life up to more happiness?

First, meditation creates more happiness through creating physical changes in the body and brain. Most notably, regular meditation can shrink the amygdala located in the brain. This is the part of the brain responsible for your most primal reactions, causing you to experience both fear and more anxiety. As this part of the brain continues to shrink over time, you will ultimately feel less of both of these unpleasant emotions. When the mind is not held captive by the negative feelings produced in the amygdala, you are likely to experience greater and more consistent levels of joy.

It is also important to discuss another phenomenon that has long fascinated researchers known as the happiness set point. This theory proposes that people are only prone to experience a certain level of happiness, and this level is determined by genetics. In other words, it states that your brain is hardwired to experience happiness only in certain capacities. This is why some people naturally seem more joyful than others, even if their life circumstances may not give them any logical reason for their joy. People who are happier have more frequent activity in the front of the brain. This activity remains fairly consistent for them, only being interrupted by stressful events for a brief period.

Fortunately, the happiness set point can be altered through regular meditation practice. If you feel that you are not experiencing the amount of happiness that you would like to feel on a daily basis, it may be time to start rewiring the brain to achieve a greater sense of happiness. Much like how meditation can shrink the amygdala and limit fear and anxiety, it can also change the interactions within the brain. This can alter the happiness set point for the better. It does this through thickening certain areas of the brain that are primarily geared toward promoting feelings of wellbeing. It can cause anxious thoughts to quiet and help melt stress away with feelings of contentment and happiness instead.

Particularly if you adopt a practice of loving-kindness meditation, you may even notice that your relationships with those around you are shifting. Because you are spending less time worrying about your own life, you will have the space to be more empathetic to others and will experience increased feelings of kindness. As your relationships start to shift to a more positive light, you will notice that you are even happier. You will no longer have to worry about strain in some of your key relationships because you can relate to friends, family members, and even partners on a much deeper and more genuine level. Meditation is good not just for you personally but also for everyone around you.

Another key benefit of adopting any type of meditation practice is the clarity that it gives you. Many people struggle with making decisions because they feel overwhelmed by all of the options in front of them. Being overwhelmed with choices and emotions makes it next to impossible to make the decision that is best for you in the long run. Meditation makes it easier by giving you the mental clarity, focus, and concentration to think through the consequences of any decision you may be faced with. Researchers have found that this practice also rewires the brain, making it easier to pay attention and process external stimuli simultaneously.

One last way that meditation can improve your happiness is through the release of chemicals that are known to have a positive effect on mood. When you sink beneath the surface of your conscious mind, your body will emit some of those chemicals that make you feel better emotionally such as serotonin and dopamine. It can also emit certain endorphins that are known to make you feel good. All of these tasks work together to make you feel better at a cellular level, boosting your mood and making your emotions more pleasant and less overwhelming.

While it is true that meditation and mindfulness practices can make you feel happier, the real question relates to how you notice those fleeting feelings of happiness. If you are used to the feelings of anxiety and worry that used to plague you, recognizing the feeling of happiness might be a challenge for you. Fortunately, you can take note of feelings of happiness and stop to appreciate them as often as you like. Try to tune into the feeling that you are living the very life you always wanted. When you start to feel at peace with the life you are living, this is a moment of happiness that you will want to tune in to. This is a sign that you are living in the moment which is always a positive thing where happiness is concerned.

Another way that you may notice moments of happiness is by stopping to take stock of everything that you are grateful for at the moment. You can start a gratitude journal (which we will talk about a little bit more at the end of this chapter) or just take a moment to list out a couple of things you are thankful for right now. If you want to give your happiness a serious boost, you can share something you are grateful for with another person in the form of a compliment or a small random act of kindness. You will feel stronger emotions when you share that internal sense of joy with others.

Take note of how well your relationships are doing. When you are truly happy, most people find that their relationships are also at peace. They may experience very little conflict in their relationships with others, though some conflict is sure to arise sometimes. Do your best to respect those around you and live a life of integrity. Pause to be grateful for the smooth sailing in your relationships or practice a session of loving-kindness meditation to send positive feelings toward the people that you are struggling with the most. Being proactive in these connections can be a great way to cultivate and take note of true happiness.

There are so many different and unique ways that you might experience pleasant feelings of happiness. Meditation and mindfulness are two ways that you can tap into this resource, but they are not the only ways you can learn to be happier. In the next section, we will cover some of the easiest and most effective ways to become a happier person.

EXERCISES TO CULTIVATE MORE HAPPINESS

Once you know how powerful happiness can be and how you can experience this emotion more fully, it is key to take a deeper look at how you can drag more happiness from the depths of your mind and body. These exercises will help you to do just that with just a few simple steps. Pick and choose which exercises will work best for you.

Gratitude Journal

Gratitude was mentioned briefly earlier in this chapter, but this is where you will start to put that muscle to good use. The very act of giving thanks for the positive things in your life helps you to reflect on the good things that happen to you – in other words, the things that make you happiest. You will experience more positivity with a commitment to the regular practice of building up this muscle. In fact, researchers have found that gratitude is tied to

resiliency, health benefits, and even stronger relationships.

Keeping a gratitude journal is a tangible way to exercise your gratitude. You can do this in a couple of
different ways. First, you can carry a small notebook
in your pocket and write down the things you are
grateful for as they come up. If this seems like too
much work or like it draws too much attention to
your happiness practice, you can list out five or ten
things that you were grateful for over the course of
the day right before you go to bed.

Some days, it might be more difficult than others to
find things you are grateful for. Think of the small
moments that occur every day that bring you joy:
a steaming cup of coffee on a cold morning, snug-
gling your puppy on the couch, or praise from your
boss. It does not matter how small or large the experience is – only that it makes you feel happy to be
alive. If you are having a hard time coming up with
specific things you are grateful for each day, you can
still be grateful for the major things like a roof over

your head, running water, and food in the refrigerator. This will still strengthen the muscle, though it is better to be as specific as possible.

Learn Something New

One of the best ways to really flex that happiness muscle is by pursuing a new and desired hobby. As you gain proficiency in something new, you will boost your self-esteem which ultimately makes you feel happier. It might take some effort to learn something new, whether it is picking up the guitar or trying a new language. However, you will find that stretching that muscle to the best of your ability can work wonders for your happiness. You do not have to be an expert to cash in on the happiness that this simple action can bring.

Find Your Tribe

Many people try to find a way around this, but it simply cannot be done. In order to be truly happy, you have to have connections with other people. Find your tribe of people who think like you, encourage you, and support you in all your future endeavors. You may not always share the exact same viewpoints and you may not see eye to eye all the time. However, growing a sense of community in your daily life is important if you want to experience a rush of neurotransmitters and endorphins.

There are no recommended numbers of friends that you should have if you want to be a happier person. Instead, it is more about the quality time that you spend with the people in your life. It does little to no good if you spend no time with the people whom you consider to be your closest friends. Set time aside each week to connect with your friends, family members, or partner in a way that feels meaningful for you. This can be different for everyone. You may choose to engage over a shared hobby, play a board game together, or simply go out for coffee and a long chat. Figure out what nourishes your soul and ask someone else to join you in that activity.

Exercise

Chances are that this is not the first time you have heard that exercise makes you a happier person. You do not have to spend hours at the gym every week to see the cumulative effects that exercise can have on your happiness. Even just a few minutes each day is enough time to really feel the difference that it can make. It makes your body stronger, increases your health, and boosts happiness all at the same time. Why wouldn't you want to try this simple activity?

Exercise releases a flood of chemicals that are known to reduce the effects of depression and cultivate happiness. It releases endorphins as well as neurotransmitters like serotonin and dopamine. It can even stimulate a hit of adrenaline to get your blood pumping and your heart racing a little faster.

There are tons of health reasons to consider exercise and gaining a sense of well-being is just the tip of the iceberg. All you have to do is put in 20 to 30 minutes of exercise and you can start to see the effects.

Set Goals for Yourself

How amazing does it feel to check something off your to-do list? Some people even write out a to-do list just for the sheer pleasure of being able to cross something off at the end of the day. One way to cultivate more happiness in your life is to set intrinsic goals for yourself. These can relate to your personal growth or even your relationships with other people. For example, you might commit to practicing a new skill until you learn something new (like learning a new song on the piano or mastering a skill in the kitchen). You might add volunteer work to your to-do list. Keep in mind that adding things to your list of goals should be about you and how it makes you feel – not what others might think about you. When you are focused on what others will think about you, these are known as extrinsic goals and do not result in the same degree of happiness found with intrinsic goals. An example of an extrinsic goal might be to make a specific improvement to your appearance or to do something major at work. While they might bring some sort of short-term happiness, intrinsic goals will foster a more long-term sense of contentment.

Rest

Have you ever woken up from a night of poor sleep and felt less than thrilled to start the day? It happens to all of us at some point. We spend all night tossing and turning or we stay up too late to watch one more episode of our favorite show. Unfortunately, the research shows that not getting enough rest can actually hamper our happiness. In general, you should strive to get at least seven to eight hours of sleep each night if you want to feel your very best.

How do you know if you need to get more sleep? If you find yourself wanting to take a nap midway through the afternoon or relying on that pot of coffee to get you through to the evening, it might be time to reevaluate your sleep habits. Try writing down how many hours of sleep you get and how you feel the following day to determine if you need to get more rest.

Smile

Did you know that pretending that you are happy may actually trigger feelings of genuine joy? Most of us smile naturally when we experience happiness, but putting a smile on when we are feeling down can also influence our overall happiness. A simple smile can release dopamine, a feel-good chemical that might have some small effect on your happiness.

This does not mean that you have to constantly pretend to be happy, even when you are feeling low. However, a brief smile every now and again can certainly help you to feel better about your life. One way you can implement this into your daily routine without feeling fake about it is to practice it when you are alone. Smile in the mirror at yourself and see what a difference it makes for your overall mood.

CONCLUSION

I t is clear that something needs to change if you truly want to experience happiness and freedom in a new capacity. Everyone can achieve these two milestones, but it will require plenty of work on your part. Happiness and being in touch with your inner voice is a practice that you must tend to and cultivate daily if you want to see long-term effects. The good news is that you do not have to spend hours a day performing complicated tasks and procedures to get a taste of what happiness is truly like for you. You can accomplish it with just a few minutes of meditation or a quick mindfulness exercise. You can implement more self-love into your daily routine by stopping the endless scrolling on social media or working in a ritual that signals care for yourself.

It does not have to be complex, and these simple actions have far-reaching effects.

For those who are determined to squeeze more happiness out of life as they know it, these are three simple keys that can help you to improve your current situation. You will learn more about yourself and your emotions, as well as develop a keener sense of hearing for that inner voice that stands out to you. Knowing what your intuition sounds like is key to helping keep your emotions in their proper place. You will not respond from a temporary feeling but from a much deeper level of knowledge that can allow you to make decisions for the long term instead. In place of making decisions based on a knee-jerk reaction, you will have more awareness of what you need out of any given situation.

Not to mention, practicing meditation, mindfulness, and self-love will allow you to tap into emotions and feelings that you may not have even been aware that you had. As you learn more about your own emotional experience, you will be more finely tuned to others and can better empathize and respond to their most pressing need for support. Even conflict will present fewer problems for you, as you will know exactly what you want out of any given situation with just a few minutes to think it over. As a result, your relationships will be much deeper and richer. This applies not only to your closest friends and family members but also to coworkers and leaders in your workplace. People may start to turn to you for advice and insight when they notice the confidence you have when making a decision.

Once you can pinpoint the feeling of happiness in your life, you will do anything to chase more of these blissful moments. There is an unending supply of happiness and freedom waiting just for you, and all you have to do is get in touch with those feelings that it can bring about. With some of these exercises, you will be well positioned to cultivate this feeling so that you can tap into it whenever you most need an infusion of happiness in your life. Whether you are in the midst of a stressful situation at work or with your children, you will be able to recognize the brief feelings of happiness that cross your path. These fleeting moments can sustain you, even in life's longest and most trying moments.

As we near the end of this book, it is important to check in with yourself and see how you are doing with your journey. Are you finding that you are able to be present at the moment, make better decisions, and experience your emotions more fully without allowing them to completely overwhelm you? Meditation and mindfulness are great for this, but self-love should not be discounted either. No matter which exercises you choose to mix and match to achieve this goal, it is more than possible for you to feel the sense of accomplishment and success that comes with these goals.

The only question that remains is: are you ready to experience more happiness and freedom in your life by listening to your inner voice and cultivating emotional intelligence? If so, then you are already on the right path to achieving a level of success that is unparalleled in your life at the moment. Examine your life for areas where you can implement these exercises and see your happiness grow exponentially.

DISCLAIMER

This book contains opinions and ideas of the author and is meant to teach the reader informative and helpful knowledge while due care should be taken by the user in the application of the information provided. The instructions and strategies are possibly not right for every reader and there is no guarantee that they work for everyone. Using this book and implementing the information/recipes therein contained is explicitly your own responsibility and risk. This work with all its contents, does not guarantee correctness, completion, quality or correctness of the provided information. Misinformation or misprints cannot be completely eliminated.

Printed in Great Britain
by Amazon